Bumper Book
of Phonics Fun

Sara Wernham and Caroline Petherbridge

© Sara Wernham, Caroline Petherbridge 2020 (text)
© Rosie Brooks (Beehive Illustration) 2020 (illustrations)
Designed & Edited by Caroline Petherbridge

With special thanks to:
John Petherbridge for writing the recipes
Summer & Daisy Petherbridge Mawdsley for making the craft

Printed in China 2020

Introduction

Welcome to the Bumper Book of Phonics Fun. It is a resource designed to support the teaching of letter sounds in a fun, multisensory way, using the world around us as a stimulus. For each sound, you will find four pages containing the following range of activities. Every activity is linked to the sound: use some or all of them in any order, depending on what is appropriate for your learners.

 Words that contain the sound within the word rather than at the beginning of it. These are often harder to hear.

 Objects or pictures to collect that connect with the sound. These can be displayed on a sound table or kept in separate boxes with the letter sound on.

 The letter sound.

 A hanging decoration related to the sound.

An idea for using either a sand or water tray.

 A baking recipe linked to the sound. The ingredients are written using metric weights and measures. Below are some conversions for those using American cups.
- Self-raising flour = 1 cup of all-purpose flour with 2 teaspoons of baking powder.
- Cornflour = Corn starch
- Flour: 120g = 1 cup
- Sugar: 200g = 1 cup
- Icing sugar: 100g = 1 cup
- Brown sugar: 180g = 1 cup
- Cornflour: 120g = 1 cup
- Butter: 240g = 1 cup
- Dried fruit: 200g = 1 cup
- Liquids: 250ml = 1 cup

 An activity that links to the sound and action being introduced. The speech bubble helps in saying the sound correctly.

 An idea for role play, drama or the home corner that is linked to the sound. A way to express imagination and creativity.

 The Jolly Phonics song lyrics and illustration for the sound being introduced. There is a Jolly Song for each sound.

The Jolly Phonics action for the sound being introduced. Encourage learners to do the action when they say or hear the sound. The movement will help to remember the sound that the letter makes.

A miniature world to build that is linked to the sound

Something new to investigate that has a link to the sound

A little extra something to try that has a link to the sound

A tongue twister to try saying quickly.

Suggestions of things to collect, investigate or look at. Discussing cross-curricular themes and extending ideas helps develop vocabulary and comprehension.

A type of music to listen to that has a link to the sound. Popular examples of music are suggested. These can always be found on YouTube.

A whiteboard and magnetic letters that show the sounds that have been taught so far. It also includes a bank of simple words that can be made using these sounds, as well as activities like matching pictures to the sounds or words. Why not have a sound table or wall as well, with plastic or wooden letters and letter cards? Encourage learners to say the sounds as they use them.

Something to look at and try to draw, either from life or from a picture.

Ideas of things to talk about that have a link to the sound

Suggestions of books or stories that have a link to the sound

An image of a word that starts with or contains the sound

Activities and crafts to make and do that have a link to the sound. A photograph and simple instructions are included.

Water Tray

Make sailing boats out of different materials and test which ones float or sink.

Sailing Boats

sink

strong

make a themed sticker collection

skeleton

Look and Draw
Draw strawberries, noticing how the seeds are on the outside.

strawberries

spaghetti

Learn how to spell out your name in sign language.

SONG (Tune: The Farmer in the Dell)

The snake is in the grass.
The snake is in the grass.
sss! sss!
The snake is in the grass.

see the sun smile sweetly

Make a sun out of a paper plate and paint it. Add paper rays.

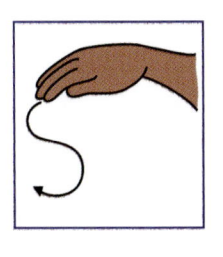
ACTION: Weave your hand in an 's' shape like a snake, and say *sssssss*.

S

Make Spiders
Make legs from pipe cleaners or folded paper. Make the body from a painted paper plate.

Think of some words that end with s.

scarecrow

Stairway to the Stars - Dexter Gordon
Soul Station - Hank Mobley

listen to saxophone music

Build a Small World

seaside

spoon

Make healthy snacks to enjoy with your friends, including sandwiches.

Can you spread, scramble, sieve, slice and stir food?

Food starting with s
salad   scone
salami   sprouts
salmon   strawberry
satsuma   sweetcorn
sausage   soup

s   s ?

make a space picture

a

Cut out arrows and make an arrow picture.

Make an Ant

a a a a

Paint two disposable spoons black and hold them together with pipe cleaners.

Spoons facing down

Bend the pipe cleaners so that the ant can stand up

anchor

antlers

Apple Cake

Ingredients:

175g soft butter
175g light brown sugar
3 eggs beaten
240g self-raising flour
1 teaspoon baking powder
1 teaspoon ground cinnamon
1/2 teaspoon ground nutmeg
350g peeled, diced cooking apples
50ml milk

Method:

Preheat oven to 160c / gas 3.
Cream butter and sugar together until smooth.
Add a spoonful of flour then slowly whisk in eggs.
Fold in rest of flour with baking powder and spices.
Stir in the apples and loosen with milk.
Pour into a lined 20cm cake tin and bake for 90 mins.

There are many different kinds of apples and they can taste quite different. Try some different varieties and find your favourite.

antenna

amphibian

OBJECTS TO COLLECT

ant
anchor
arrow
apple
ambulance
alligator

apple

discover how we celebrate anniversaries with flowers

1st PANSY   2nd COSMOS   3rd FUCHSIA   4th GERANIUM   5th DAISY

6th CALLA LILY   7th JACK-IN-THE-PULPIT   8th CLEMATIS   9th POPPY   10th DAFFODIL

Role Play

Be actors in your very own theatre. Produce your own play or musical.

Build a Small World →

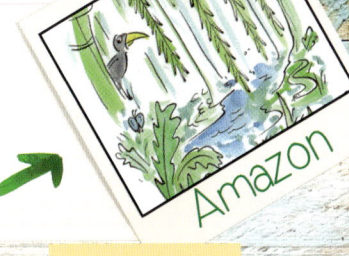

Amazon

The Amazon is a rainforest in South America.

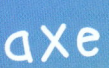

axe

SONG (Tune: Skip to My Lou)

a-a! a-a! Ants on my arm.
a-a! a-a! Ants on my arm.
a-a! a-a! Ants on my arm.
They're causing me alarm.

Cut apples in half and print patterns.

ACTION: Wiggle your fingers up your arm as if ants are crawling on you, and say *a, a, a, a!*

acrobat

atlas

Water Tray

Make anchors out of different materials and see which ones sink and which ones float.

foil floats
playdough sinks

Anchors

What materials absorb water? Experiment and find out! Try:

cotton ball
paper
foil
plastic bag
sponge
facecloth
tissue
polystyrene
cardboard
glass
metal
wool

Make an Astronaut

Yogurt pot helmet →

Use a Ping-Pong ball for a head

Paint a cardboard tube white

Cut out cardboard arms and legs

BOOKS TO READ

Ants - Jolly Readers

Ant & Bee Series
 - Angela Banner

Ants in Your Pants!
 - Julia Jarman

Alfie books
 - Shirley Hughes

Anansi the Spider
 - Folk Story

Animalia
 - Graeme Base

Ten Apples Up on Top
 - Dr. Seuss

Talk about activities you do outside school.

Talk about your ambitions in life.

Talk about what makes you angry.

Sand Tray

Make a treasure map in the sand tray. You can use stones, shells, sticks. Add an X to mark the spot!

Treasure

Hear the /t/ in
caterpillar
nest
ant

Play with a tennis ball. Practise throwing and catching.

Design your own tattoo. Make it personal to you.

Paint the same tree in the four different seasons.

What is your favourite season for trees? Do you like the blossom of spring, the colours of autumn, the green of summer or the bare branches of winter?

SONG (Tune: The Muffin Man)

When I watch the tennis game,
t - t - t,
t - t - t...
...when I watch the tennis game,
my head goes back and forth.

teeth

tricycle

ACTION: Turn your head from side to side as if you are watching tennis, and say t, t, t.

Build a Small World →

town

i

make your own Italian pizza

What are your favourite pizza toppings?

ill

Make Inkblot Pictures

Turn black splodges into anything!

iiii

index finger

infant

Italian Gelato Cake

Ingredients:

350ml double cream
50g dark chocolate splintered
110g meringue nests crushed

For the Sauce:
100ml double cream
50g dark chocolate
200g fresh raspberries

Method:

Line a 1 litre loaf tin with cling film (leave enough to cover the top).
Whisk double cream into firm peaks and stir in splintered chocolate and crushed meringue.
Spoon into loaf tin, cover with cling film and freeze for at least 4 hours.
For the sauce, warm up cream and melt in the chocolate.
Serve cake sliced with a spoonful of sauce and some fresh raspberries.

Paint Italian penne pasta and thread onto string or wool to make a necklace.

OBJECTS TO COLLECT

inflatable toys
ink pen
inhaler
indigo objects

itch

find out about different types of Italian pasta.

farfalle
penne
tagliatelle
rigatoni
conchiglie
fusilli
stortini
rigatoni
spaghetti
macaroni
linguine

Role Play

Be magicians and put on magic shows featuring clever illusions.

Build a Small World →

Italy

injury

SONG (Tune: Hickory Dickory Dock)

Inky the mouse is my pet.
She spilled the ink and got wet.
The ink it spread
all over the desk.
/i/ - /i/ - /i/ - /i/
- Inky's wet!

Make an igloo.

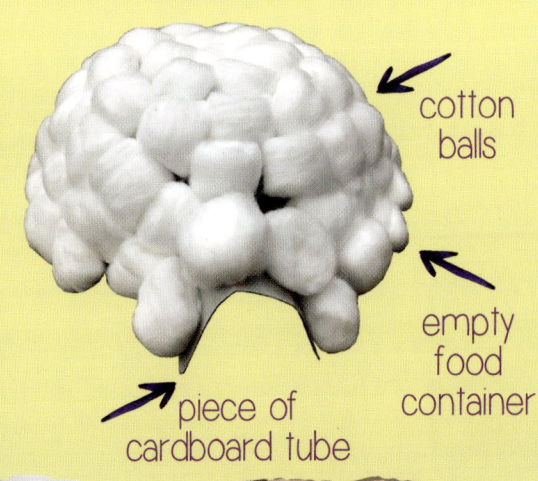

cotton balls
empty food container
piece of cardboard tube

ACTION: Wiggle your fingers at the end of your nose as if you are a mouse stroking its whiskers and squeak i, i, i, i.

inside
indoors

17

i

Tongue Twister
The insects had an interesting illness that made them itchy.

What other words have an /i/ sound?

Hear the /i/ in

sip · sit · spill

Look at the illustrations in lots of different picture books. How are they different? Who is your favourite illustrator?

Investigate:
Quentin Blake
Ernest Shepard
Beatrix Potter
Raymond Briggs
Axel Scheffler

An inchworm is the larva of a moth.

Find out about:
woodwind instruments
stringed instruments
brass instruments
percussion instruments

Look and Draw
Look at pictures of inchworms and try to draw one. They are very small!

inchworm

information

listen to instruments in an orchestra

Make an Interesting Headband

Use craft feathers

Colourful designs

Play a sound-matching pairs game.

s a t i
make words

at sat
it sit

Sand Tray

Push objects into wet sand to make impressions. Can you guess the object from the impression?

Impressions

invitation

What are the inititals of your name?

Make Insects

Use paper plates to make all these minibeasts.

BOOKS TO READ

Inch and Grub
- Alastair Chisholm & David Roberts

Just Imagine
- Pippa Goodhart

The Witch with an Itch
- Helen Baugh & Deborah Allwright

Mr. Impossible
- Roger Hargreaves

Talk about any injuries you have had.

Talk about things that interest you.

Do impressions of people you know.

Make a refreshing fruit salad with fruits that start with /p/.

How many of the fruits have you tried before?

P Fruits
plum
pineapple
peach
pear
passion fruit
papaya

Role Play

Put on a puppet show. Hang up a curtain to hide behind as the puppets perform.

Water Tray

Make a pirate ship to sail in the water tray. Use materials that float well. How many coins can you balance on top?

pirate ship

SONG (Tune: The Wheels on the Bus)

Puff out the candles on the pink pink cake.
/p/-/p/-/p/,
/p/-/p/-/p/.
Puff out the candles on the pink pink cake.
Puff! Puff! Puff!

Make a peacock. Stick feathers behind a cardboard body. As colourful as you like.

ACTION: Hold up your finger as if it is a candle and pretend to puff it out, saying p, p, p, p.

parachute

Peter Piper picked a peck of pickled peppers.

Build a Small World

pond

Sand Tray

Use your finger to write numbers in the sound tray. Practice makes perfect!

Numbers

Tongue Twister
Nine nervous nightingales made nine neat nests.

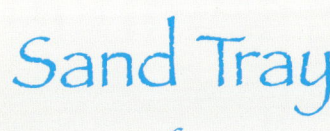
newt

create some nail designs

Draw around your hands first

net

Look and Draw
Crack open some nut shells and draw what the nuts look like inside.

nuts

nectar

Make up nonsense rhymes.

SONG (Tune: Skip to My Lou)

Hear the aeroplane, /nnn/!
Hear the aeroplane, /nnn/!
Hear the aeroplane, /nnn/!...
...making lots of noise.

ACTION: Pretend to be a plane with your arms out like wings, and say *nnnnnn*.

Make a night time picture

make a collection of nuts

Compare their:
colour
size
texture
shape

Take care if people have nut allergies!

Types of nuts:
pistachio   peanut
hazelnut   pecan
cashew   pine nut
walnut   macadamia
almond   coconut

neighbours

make a nest

Use craft leaves or real leaves.

Stick on any scraps of material or paper that you can find

BOOKS TO READ

Nursery Rhymes

Not Now Bernard
 - David McKee

What Noise Does a Rabbit Make?
 - Carrie Weston

The Last Noo-Noo
 - Jill Murphy

The Napping House
 - Audrey Wood

The Nutcracker and the Mouse King
 - E.T.A. Hoffmann

Talk about your night time routine.

Talk about your fun nicknames.

Talk about your latest news.

c k

Make a kite with a colourful design and a tail.

ribbon and felt

clock

Check the calendar. What is the date today?

Make Castanets

c k ck ck

← Fold circles of card in half and colour brightly.

↑ Stick metal bottle tops on the top and bottom.

camel

Sing 'My Grandfather's Clock'

Carrot Cake

Ingredients:
- 170g sugar
- 120ml vegetable oil
- 2 beaten eggs
- 150g plain flour
- 1 teaspoon baking soda
- 1 teaspoon ground cinnamon
- 200g grated carrot
- 1 teaspoon grated ginger
- 50g walnut pieces
- 50g soaked raisins
- 5g almond powder
- zest of 1 lemon

Method:
Preheat oven to 180c / gas 4.
Whisk together the sugar, oil and eggs until all the sugar is dissolved.
Sieve in the flour, soda and cinnamon and stir well.
Fold in the remaining ingredients.
Pour into a greased, lined 22cm cake tin and bake for 45 mins.

camera

kangaroo

OBJECTS TO COLLECT
- kite
- camera
- castanets
- kilt
- keyboard
- kiwi

koala

make a collection of coins from the past

HALF PENCE

HALF A CROWN PENNY FARTHING

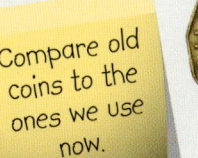

THREEPENCE ROMAN COINS

Compare old coins to the ones we use now.

Role Play

Be cooks in the kitchen. Serve up delicious food for your friends and family.

Build a Small World

camp site

canvas

Make a colour wheel

use the 7 colours of the rainbow

spin the wheel and watch colours appear and disappear

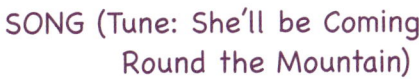

SONG (Tune: She'll be Coming Round the Mountain)

We are clicking castanets,
/c/-/c/-/c/.
We are clicking castanets,
/c/-/c/-/c/.
We are clicking castanets,
clicking castanets...
...we are clicking castanets,
/c/-/c/-/c/.

Kites are flying in the sky,
/k/-/k/-/k/.
Kites are flying in the sky,
/k/-/k/-/k/.
Kites are flying in the sky,
flying in the sky...
...Kites are flying in the sky,
/k/-/k/-/k/.

ACTION: Snap your fingers together in the air as if you are playing castanets, and say
c, k, ck, ck.

cat kittens

c k

Tongue Twister
The careless kipper caught a cold from a cool crawling crab.

kettle

Look at animals that use camouflage. Why do they want to hide in the background?
leopard, snake, frog, lizard

Look and Draw
Cacti come in all shapes, sizes and colours. Try drawing one.

cacti

Make a caterpillar
Use pipe cleaners for the antennae

Make the body with paper chains.

Sing, Sing, Sing - Benny Goodman
Mozart's Clarinet Quintet K581 - Sabine Meyer

listen to clarinet music

make a collection of keys

s a t i p n c k

make words

cat, cap, can, act, ink
kit, kin, kip, kiss
kick, tick, pick, nick
pack, tack, sack, stick
skip, skin, sick
picnic

kick
•••

sack
•••

pack
•••

When 2 letters that make the same sound come together, only say the sound once.

30

What can you do to help the environment? Cut down on single-use plastics? Walk instead of taking the car?

Single-Use Plastic
plastic shopping bags
plastic straws
plastic cups
plastic bottles
plastic cutlery
plastic lids

Role Play

Be the editor of a class newspaper. Choose articles to include and take photos.

Sand Tray

In the tray are some whole eggs and some egg shells. Hide a coin under one egg shell. Who can find the coin first?

egg game

SONG (Tune: Skip to My Lou)

Eggs in the pan, /e/-/e/-/e/.
Eggs in the pan, /e/-/e/-/e/.
Eggs in the pan, /e/-/e/-/e/.
Crack the egg
like this.../e/!

Make a poster to highlight something you can do to help the environment.

crushed tissue paper for a 3-D effect.

ACTION: Pretend to crack an egg against the side of a pan with one hand. Use both hands to open the shell, saying e, e, e, e.

empty

Sing the song 'Nellie the Elephant'.

Build a Small World

education

e

Tongue Twister
Emily excitedly ate eight excellent eggs with effort.

exercise

try eggs cooked different ways
- scrambled
- boiled
- fried
- poached

entrance

exit

Make your own envelope out of a sheet of paper (take an envelope apart to see how it folds together).

Write your address and design a stamp

Nimrod
Land of Hope and Glory
Enigma Variations

Edward Elgar
1857-1934

listen to music by composer Edward Elgar

Hear the /e/ in
- hen
- net
- pen

Play an Echo Game
Someone makes a sound or does an action and each player in turn echoes it and passes it on. When it reaches the last person, has it changed?

Make a moving elbow joint
Use a split pin for the joint

s a t i p n c k e

Make words
set, ten, pen, pet, net
peck, neck
tent, sent, test, pest
nest, step, tennis
insect

Sound out words

h

make a hippo from two paper plates

What fun things do you do to try and stop hiccups?

happy

hair

Play Hopscotch

Hopping helps your balancing skills.

hhhh

Use chalk to draw squares and numbers on the ground

Hummingbird Cake

Ingredients:
350g self-raising flour
1 teaspoon ground cinnamon
350g golden sugar
4 ripe bananas
425g chopped pineapple chunks
2 eggs beaten
180ml olive oil
1 teaspoon vanilla extract

For the Topping:
400g icing sugar
150g soft butter
200g cream cheese

Method:
Preheat oven to 180c / gas 4.
Sieve flour and cinnamon into a large bowl and stir in sugar.
In another bowl, mash bananas and add pineapple, eggs and oil. Mix well and fold into the flour.
Divide into 2 x 2lcm lined cake tins and bake for 40 mins.
Beat sugar, butter and cream cheese together to make the topping, spread on each cooled cake and stand on top of each other.

Role Play

Be heroes with powers to help others and fight crime!

helicopter

OBJECTS TO COLLECT

hairbrush
hammer
heart
honey jar
helicopter
hay

Water Tray

Make a harbour in the water tray. Make small boats from bottle lids and collect some stones.

Harbour

make a house
Cut the top off a juice or milk carton.

Make a collage of hot things.

sun
volcano
fire
oven
engine
steam

Find out

find out which foods are harvested from the fields

grains   fruits   vegetables

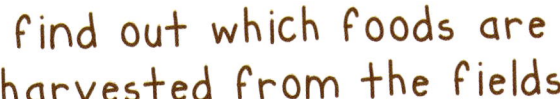

wheat   pumpkin   potatoes

SONG (Tune: Apples and Bananas)

I like to hop, hop, hop, up and down.
I like to hop, hop, hop, all around.
I like to hop, hop, hop, up and down -
/h/-/h/-/h/-/h/-/h/!

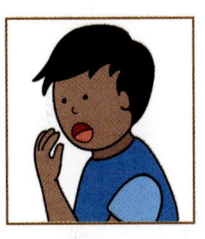

ACTION: Hold your hand up to your mouth as if you are out of breath, and say h, h, h, h.

Find out which animals hibernate in the winter.

What happens at Halloween?

Build a Small World →

home

Tongue Twister

Henry the happy hamster had a hutch for a home.

Use hexagons to make a honeycomb

You can use pom-poms to make bees

Make footprint horses

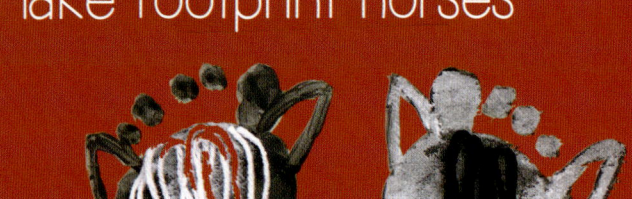

Use a black felt-tip pen to add detail.

Stick on wool to make a mane.

Look and Draw
Look at your hand and try drawing the shapes and lines you see.

hands

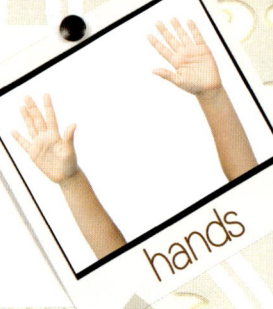

hatch

bank vole

dormouse

Discover why hedgerows are important to wildlife and why we need to protect them

harvest mouse

hedgehog

Which animals rely on hedgerows?

Bats and butterflies use hedgerows as paths when they fly.

s a t i p
n ck e h

Fill in missing letters

t __en 10
h __en
p __en
t __ent

Make words

hat, hen, hip
hit,
hack, hiss
hint

handkerchief

hammer

38

Sand Tray

Use a rake in the sand tray and make lines and patterns. Wet sand works better than dry.

Rake

Tongue Twister
The rhino and the reindeer ran a race down the road.

radio

recipe

Look and Draw
Look at yourself in the mirror and draw your reflection.

reflection

Make a robot

Use any old boxes or packaging that you have.

reading

Robins are around all year, not just in the winter.

SONG (Tune: The Muffin Man)

See my puppy rip the rag /rrr/! /rrr/!
See my puppy rip the rag, when he pulls so hard.

ACTION: Pretend to be a puppy pulling a rag and shake your head from side to side, saying *rrrrrr*.

Make a robin from two paper bowls

r

a rainbow has 7 colours

Paint a rainbow

red
orange
yellow
green
blue
indigo
violet

Red colours:
ruby
maroon
scarlet
crimson

rose

Roman

Try playing a recorder yourself. See how many different notes you can make.

listen to a recorder

Build a Small World

rocket

Find out what rubbish you can recycle. Check you know which recycling bin is which.

cardboard, paper, foil, tin can, glass

strawberries
raspberries
cherries
cranberries
red currants

s a t i p
n ck e h r

Say each sound as quickly as you can.

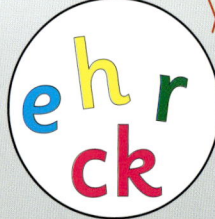

Make words
rat, rap, rip, ran
rack, rant, rest
press, print, risk
scrap, track, strap
trick, trip, crisp

Never eat wild berries without checking what they are.

eat healthy red berries

Sand Tray

Pile up the sand to make a mountain and surround it with stones and plant cuttings.

Mountain

Tongue Twister

Meg mixed milk and mustard and made a mess on the mat.

use a magnet to see if objects are metal

mat

mechanic

Look and Draw
Draw some different types of melon. Notice the patterns on the skin.

melons

medicine

Name the months of the year.

SONG (Tune: The Wheels on the Bus)

The mum and dad make many meals. /mmm/! /mmm/!
The mum and dad make many meals for their hungry children.

Turn your handprint into a monkey

Stick on googly eyes

ACTION: Rub your tummy as if you can see some tasty food, and say *mmmmmm*.

45

m

Make a mole in a hole!

Cut a slit in the tights

Cut the bottom out of an old flower pot and cover with an old pair of tights

Paint a wooden spoon black and stick on a nose and paws

It pops out of the hole!

magazine

monkey

magnifying glass

Kentucky Mandolin — Bill Monroe
Mandolin Insanity — Marty Stuart

listen to mandolin music

Build a Small World

market

The artist L.S. Lowry was famous for painting people called 'matchstick men' in his artwork.

Look at this painting, called 'Coming Out of School'.

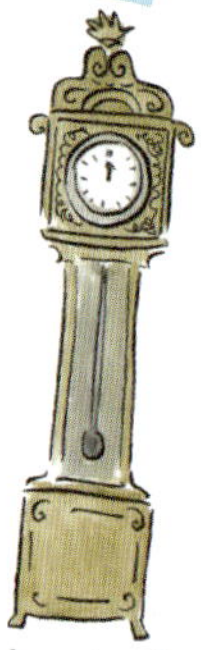

midnight

s a t i p n
ck e h r m

What is the end sound?

te _   10
he _
ca _
si _

Make words

mat, map, man, men
him, rim, hem, ram, tram
mess, miss, mist, mint
camp, stamp, pram, stem

make your own matchstick men

Sand Tray

Dig for diamonds in the sand tray. Use glass nuggets or fake jewels. How many can be found?

Diamonds

Tongue Twister
The dress was decorated with delicate diamonds.

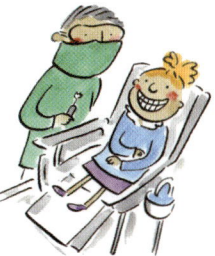
dentist

Make doughnut decorations

Use saltdough and bake in the oven.

Then paint and decorate with glitter and sequins.

SALTDOUGH RECIPE: Mix together equal amounts of plain flour, salt and water.

den

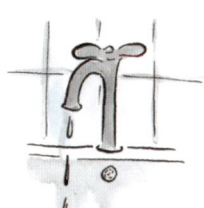
drip

Dice are made of 6 squares that make a cube.

Look and Draw
Design patterns that make good decorations for clothes or wallpaper.

design

SONG (Tune: This Old Man)

See me play on my drum.
Playing drums is lots of fun,
with a /d/-/d/-/d/-/d/
/d/-/d/-/d/-/d/-/d/.
See me play
upon my drum!

ACTION: Move your hands up and down as if you are beating a drum, and say, d, d, d, d.

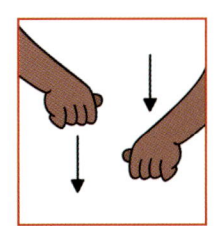

Make dice with numbers or pictures.

Picture dice can help inspire storytelling.

try fruit you may not have tried before

dragon fruit

Why do you think it is named after a dragon?

damson

Try damson jam too. Damsons are a variety of plum.

dictionary

dirty

dolphin

Do you know what the date is today?

Make a daffodil picture

BOOKS TO READ

Puff the Magic Dragon
 - Peter Yarrow
   & Lenny Lipton

Dinosaur Roar
 - Henrietta Stickland

Dogger
 - Shirley Hughes

Hairy Maclary from
  Donaldson's Dairy
 - Lynley Dodd

Diary of a Wimpy Kid
 - Jeff Kinney

That's Not my Dinosaur
 - Usborne

Talk about your favourite dessert.

Talk about special dates in the year.

Talk about going to the doctors.

g

make a greeting card collection

Cut up old greeting cards and make collages with them.

Make a Gurgling Sink

- paper straw
- gggg
- use a tissue box
- egg box sections
- cardboard tube

game

goal

Do you wear goggles when you are swimming?

gallery

Gooseberry Cake

Ingredients:
- 225g soft butter
- 225g golden caster sugar
- 200g self-raising flour
- 50g ground almonds
- 4 eggs beaten
- 1 orange zested and juiced
- 225g fresh gooseberries, topped and tailed
- 150g caster sugar

Method:
Preheat oven to 180c / gas 4.
Whisk together the butter, golden sugar, flour, orange zest and almonds until smooth.
Tip in three quarters of the gooseberries and mix well. Pour into a lined 25 x 25cm baking tin.
Gently push in the remaining gooseberries and bake for 30 mins.
Meanwhile, sieve the orange juice and mix in the caster sugar. Spoon the syrup over the cake and bake for 5 more mins.

make a paper plate goose

OBJECTS TO COLLECT

- goat
- green things
- globe
- grapes
- gorilla
- garlic

tomato

bean

Try growing your own fruit and vegetables. You could try to grow your favourites.

Have you tried these fruits?
grapes
guava
grapefruit
gooseberry
galia melon

Role Play
Be a greengrocer and set up lots of healthy fruit and vegetables to sell to customers.

Water Tray
Put sand on the bottom of the water tray and use a sieve to pan for gold nuggets. Try to find ten pieces.

gold

SONG (Tune: Jimmy Crack Corn)

The water gurgles
 down the drain.
The water gurgles
 down the drain.
The water gurgles
 down the drain,
/g/ -/g/ -/g/
 -/g/ -/g/.

ACTION: Move your hand in a downward spiral like water gurgling down a drain, and say g, g, g, g.

Make a globe.
Cover a balloon with strips of textured paper towels dipped in a PVA glue & water mixture.

When dry, sponge on blue and green paint.

goblet

gloves

Build a Small World

garden

Sand Tray

Make a beautiful underwater Octopus's Garden with brightly coloured plants.

Octopus's Garden

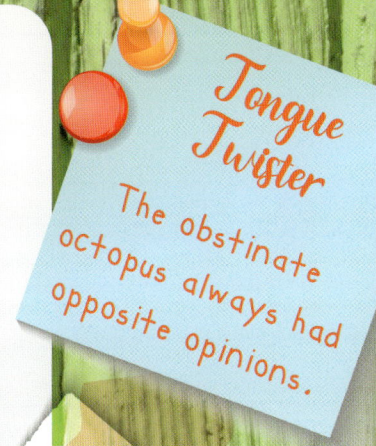
Tongue Twister
The obstinate octopus always had opposite opinions.

observation

Make an octopus

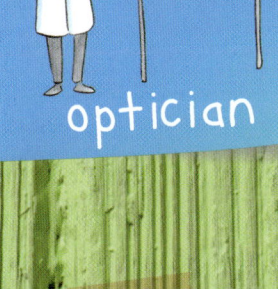
optician

Look and Draw
Make a still life arrangement and do an observational drawing of it.

observation

operation

SONG (Tune: Old MacDonald)

Now it's dark,
  the lights go on.
/o/-/o/-/o/-/o/-/o/.
Time for bed,
  the lights go off!
/o/-/o/-/o/-/o/-/o/.

paper chains

ACTION: Pretend to turn a light switch on and off, and say *o-o, o-o*.

Play a game of opposites

small   big   wet   dry

sad   happy   young   old

57

What can you find in the undergrowth of a forest or wood? Look for:

ferns, moss, fungi, flowers

unfit

Role Play

Be an undercover detective and solve mysteries and crimes.

compare unhealthy and healthy food

SONG (Tune: Skip to My Lou)

/u/-/u/ up go umbrellas.
/u/-/u/ up go umbrellas.
/u/-/u/ up go umbrellas...
...when it starts to rain!

Try using:
leaves
pasta
seeds
buttons
ribbon
cotton

Make an underground collage

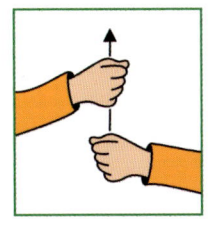

ACTION: Keep one hand steady and raise the other as if putting up an umbrella, and say u, u, u, u.

upset

Build a Small World

underground

u

underneath

unlucky

Make an ugly duckling

feathers · half a paper plate

Tongue Twister
Unluckily, my uncle is unlikely to fit under the umbrella.

This famous story is written by Hans Christian Andersen

listen to the story of The Ugly Duckling

Hear the /u/ in

mug   cup

unravel

Hear the /u/ in

hut

bun

sun

s a t i p n
c k e h r m d
g o u

Make words

up, rug, sun, hut, nut, mud
run, cup, pump, cut, tug
mug, stuck, duck, crust

Which vowel sound?

| u | i |

| a | |
| e | o |

l

What can be liquid and solid?
egg   water   chocolate

Try some experiments to turn liquids to solids.

lamb

ladder

Make a Lollipop
Decorate in any pattern you like.
Use sequins and glitter glue to decorate.

Lemon Cake
Ingredients:
- 5 eggs beaten
- 300g sugar
- 140ml double cream
- finely grated zest of 3 lemons
- 80g butter, melted
- 240g plain flour
- half teaspoon baking powder

For the Glaze:
- 50g apricot jam warmed
- finely grated zest of 1 lemon
- 3 tablespoons lemon juice
- 150g icing sugar

Method:
Preheat oven to 180c / gas 4.
Whisk together the eggs, sugar, cream, zest and melted butter.
Sift flour and baking powder together then whisk into the egg mixture until smooth.
Pour into greased loaf tin and bake for 55 mins. After 10 mins, spread top of cake with jam.
Gently heat lemon zest, juice and icing sugar, stirring continuously. When smooth, spoon glaze over the cake.

Role Play
Be a librarian in a library. Help people find books they will enjoy reading.

lamp

OBJECTS TO COLLECT
letters
laces
lemon
leaves
lizard
labels

Sand Tray

Make a collection of lids and use them in the sand tray to make a picture or collage.

Lids

Tongue Twister
The lazy lion liked loafing and lying around the lake.

llama luggage

Make a lantern

Fold a piece of paper in half and make cuts along the folded edge, but not all the way to the end.

Open the paper and bring the long sides together to make a tube.

Add a strip of paper for a handle.

lock

log

Look and Draw
Draw the jagged patterns forked lightning makes when it strikes.

lightning

Can you tie your own shoelaces?

SONG (Tune: The Farmer in the Dell)

We lick our lollipops.
We lick our lollipops.
/l/-/l/-/l/-/l/!
We lick our lollipops.

ACTION: Pretend to lick a lollipop, saying /lllll/.

Make leaf prints with paint and dry leaves

Sprinkle glitter on the print before it dries

Make different faces in the mirror and draw the expressions.

How many different faces can be made?

Fun F Verbs
fishing fixing
flying   farming
falling filling
filming fluttering
fussing folding

Role Play

Make a fruit market stall. Name, weigh, taste, buy and sell all kinds of fruit.

Sand Tray

Make sandcastles with flags in. Collect sticks to paint and use any kind of paper.

flags

SONG (Tune: Old MacDonald)

My friends and I went to the beach with my floating fish.
It got a hole...
...the air came out.
ffffff!

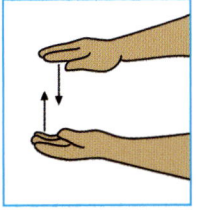

ACTION: Slowly bring your hands together to mime an inflatable fish deflating, and say ffffff.

five fat frogs full of fun

Make a frog out of a folded paper plate and paint it.

factory

Build a Small World

farm

69

Water Tray

Play with bottles in the water tray. Fill and empty them. Which bottle holds the most water?

Bottles

Tongue Twister
Billy Bear was badly behaved and busy being a bully.

batteries

Make bells

cut the top off a plastic bottle and paint it gold

butter

Why is good behaviour important?

Look and Draw
Look at the patterns on a butterfly's wings and draw your own.

butterfly

barbecue

SONG (Tune: Camptown Races)
Bring your bat and bring your ball. /b/-/b/!
Bring your bat and bring your ball...
...to the park to play!

Make binoculars

Use two cardboard tubes stuck together and stick on some string so you can wear them around your neck

ACTION: Pretend to hit a ball with a bat, saying b, b, b, b.

73

b

Decorate letters with buttons

Try making the letter that starts your name.

bride

balloons

Dueling Banjos – Eric Weissberg & Steve Mandell

listen to banjo music

Build a Small World

birthday party

Look at photos of you when you were a baby.

basket

Try baking your own bread. It's not very difficult and you don't need many ingredients.

 flour
 salt
 water
 yeast

s a t i p n
c k e h r m d
g o u l f b

Make words

bat, ban, bad, bag, bet, bed
beg, bit, bin, bid, big, but, bun
bud, bug, back, crab, grab, club
rabbit, bulb, bump, band, bend
belt, black, brick

Play bingo

a	sip	🥮
sad	🌹	e
🧸	i	pat
r	rip	🪁
pet	🪭	h
☀	s	mat

make bead bracelets

ai

Make a train using old boxes and cardboard tubes.

trainers

afraid

Make Listening Ears

Use modelling dough

ai?

Raisin Honey Loaf Cake

Ingredients:

  300g self-raising flour
  1/2 teaspoon salt
  1 teaspoon ground ginger
  100g soft butter
  60g sugar
  200g raisins
  2 tablespoons honey
  1 egg beaten
  100ml milk (room temperature)

Method:

  Preheat oven to 180c / gas 4.
  Place flour, salt, ginger and butter in a food processor and mix until it resembles fine breadcrumbs.
  Move into a mixing bowl and mix with sugar and raisins.
  Add honey, eggs and milk and mix until soft.
  Pour into a greased loaf tin and bake for 35 mins.
  Loosely cover with foil and bake for a further 35 mins.

Role Play

Be a children's party entertainer. Do tricks, sing and dance and tell jokes.

Go on a listening walk and make a note of all the sounds you hear.

brain

OBJECTS TO COLLECT

train
sail boat
snail
nail polish
paint
raisins

Can you hear the same sound?

whale day cake scales

Make a daisy chain

Make daisies from white and yellow card and stick them onto a ribbon.

make fruit cocktails

Blend your favourite fruits with crushed ice

Have you ever painted your nails?

Make a raindrop mobile

Write words with an /ai/ sound inside each raindrop.

rain, aim, train, nail, sail, brain

SONG (Tune: Camptown Races)

My ear hurt.
I was in pain.
/ai/? /ai/?

My ear hurt.
I was in pain.
What did you try to say?

ACTION: Cup your hand over your ear as if you are trying to hear something, and say *ai*?

first aid

braids

Build a Small World

mermaid cave

ai

Tongue Twister
I must explain why I failed again to email and complain.

Stick squares of paper in patterns to make a mosaic.

The Romans liked to make mosaics of people, animals, birds and fish.

Look and Draw
Look at the shapes and patterns on a snail shell and try drawing some.

toenails

snail shell

Sorting office — mail van

airmail

Find out what happens to mail once you have posted it. Have you ever posted an airmail letter to another country?

Mix paints to make different colours. What other colours can you make from blue, yellow, red and green paint?

snail

stain

What does a tailor use?

When two letters come together to make one sound it is called a digraph.

Say the sounds while pointing to the dots.

ai

Make words

aid, hail, pail, pain, gain, paid
main, bait, nail, tail, sail, fail
rail, train, brain, drain, paint
sprain, maid, claim, stain
grain, saint

ai m
r ai n

make paper chains

j

make a collection of jewels

javelin

judo

Make a Jelly

j j j j

use jelly cubes

watch it wobble!

Fake jewels can look just as good as real ones! Can you tell the difference?

Around the world, this wobbly dessert is known as either jelly or jello. Which do you say?

Jaffa Cakes
Ingredients:
1 x 135g pack of orange jelly cubes
150g boiling water
3 tablespoons orange marmalade
1 egg beaten
25g sugar
25g plain flour
175g chocolate (30-40% cocoa) melted & slightly cooled

Method:
Preheat oven to 180c / gas 4.
Place jelly and marmalade in a bowl and cover with the boiling water. Stir until smooth.
Line a 22cm cake tin with plastic wrap and pour in the mixture. Refrigerate until set.
In another bowl, whisk the egg and sugar well. Fold in the sieved flour. Spoon a tablespoon of dough into each of the 12 holes of a bun tin. Smooth the tops and bake for 8 mins.
Use a ring cutter to cut the set jelly into 12 circles. Lay the jelly on the cooled cakes and pour the chocolate over them. Refrigerate to set.

jack-in-the-box

Make a jellyfish

paint a bowl

cut strips of bubble wrap and tissue paper

frog
boa constrictor
lizard
tiger
gorilla
Which animals do you find in the jungle? Find out which ones are endangered

jaguar

Role Play
Be a judge in court and help settle arguments.

taste different flavours of jam

Which is your favourite?

SONG (Tune: Jingle Bells)
Jelly and jam,
jelly and jam,
jiggling on the plate.
Oh, what will
I eat with it?
/j/ - /j// j/ - /j// j/.

ACTION: Pretend to wobble like a jelly on a plate, saying j, j, j, j.

Make Japanese dolls

use origami paper

Do a jigsaw puzzle.

Build a Small World

jungle

j

Tongue Twister
John the joyful juggler jumped with joy whilst he juggled

Make your own jigsaw puzzle from a painting or drawing you have done.

Make a jukebox

start with a box and decorate it with mini records and rock & roll images

If you had a jukebox, what songs would you put on it?

jacket

jury

Another Day of Sun - La La Land
In the Mood - Glenn Miller

listen to jazz music

juggle

jet

find out about the planet Jupiter

It is the largest planet in our solar system and is made of gas. It has a giant red spot that is a raging storm.

s a t i p n
c k e h r m d
g o u l f b
a i j

Write sounds on large cards and put them around the room. Call out a sound and see who can JUMP to it first.

ai   u
j   n

Make words
jam, jump, jet, just
jab, job, jail, jog, jug, jut

Can you hear the same sound?

bone
rose
snowman
globe

lifeboat

toast

Try roasting some vegetables.

Make a soap foam print

Mix some washing liquid with a little water and some water-based paint. Blow into it with a straw to make foam. Keep blowing until the bubbles spill out of the bowl and onto a piece of white paper. Then leave to dry.

Make a foam shape picture

Draw shapes and cut them out.

SONG (Tune: The Muffin Man)

Oh, did you see the billy goat?
/oa/-/oa/-/oa/, /oa/-/oa/-/oa/
Oh, did you see the billy goat,
under the old oak tree?

ACTION: Bring your hand over your mouth as if something has gone wrong, and say *oa*!

download

roast

Build a Small World

coast

ie

make a bow tie collection

Can you tie a neck tie yourself?

spies

Make a Sailor

Use anything from nature that you can find outside: acorns, conkers, seeds, seed cases and berries.

ie-ie

Hold things together with toothpicks and string.

Apple Pie
Ingredients:

375g ready rolled puff pastry
1 egg yolk beaten
3 tablespoons cold water
3 large cooking apples peeled, cored and chopped
50g sugar

Method:

Preheat oven to 200c / gas 6.
Heat the apple pieces in a covered pan with the water. Stew and stir regularly until the apple is soft. Let it cool down and add the sugar.
Roll out half of the pastry and cover the base of a greased 20cm pie dish. Pour in the apple and then trim the edges.
Roll out the other half of the pastry, moisten the edges and lay on top. Pinch down around the edges to seal and trim.
Make fork holes all over the top and paint with the egg yolk.
Bake for 30 mins.

Role Play

Be parents with a baby that cries. How do you care for the baby?

flies

DRESS UP AS SPIES
smart jacket
smart trousers
white shirt
black tie
sunglasses

ie

Tongue Twister
The spies tried to eat fries until they were satisfied.

Make a carton of fries
sponge
MY FRIES
This template will make the carton.

Can you tie your own shoelaces?

Look and Draw
Look at the skies around you at different times of the day and draw what you see.

skies

Find out about magpies. They are known as "thieving magpies" but they don't really steal shiny things. It's a myth!

dies

Listen to the cries of different animals. Which animals make which sounds?

Animal Cries
whinny   bellow
screech   bleat
chatter   howl
hoot   roar
bark   moo
croak   shriek
hiss   whine

butterflies

s a t i p n
c k e h r m d
g o u l f b
ai j oa ie

Play a game of eye-spy
"I spy with my little eye, something beginning with..."

Make words
tie, pie, lie, die,
cried, fried, spied
tried, died, lied, dried
untie, magpie

Try tie-dying a T-shirt
Roll or scrunch a white T-shirt and secure with rubber bands
Use a tie-dye kit and follow the instructions carefully. Try rolling and scrunching it differently to create different patterns.

try eating dried fruit

- apricot
- banana
- mango
- papaya
- sultanas

try making your own dried fruit

Wash and dry the fruit and cut into very thin slices. Lay the pieces separately on a lined baking sheet and bake in the oven on the lowest setting for 4 to 8 hours. Fruits take different amounts of time — just check the fruit is shriveling up without burning.

It flies!

- helicopter
- butterfly
- bee
- plane
- bird
- kite

pie

Make symmetrical butterflies

Paint only half of the butterfly and then fold it over to print the other symmetrical wing.

flies

BOOKS TO READ

The Apple Pie Tree
- Zoe Hall

Winnie Flies Again
- Valerie Thomas & Korky Paul

Bear Flies High
- Michael Rosen

Mince Spies
- Mark Sperring & Sophie Corrigan

When Someone Very Special Dies
- Marge Heegaard

Talk about why you shouldn't tell lies.

Talk about new foods you've tried.

Talk about your favourite pie.

Can you hear the same sound?

tea
peas
donkey
leaves

make a healthy green smoothie

you can try blending some of these:

kiwi
lime
apple
pear
avocado
spinach
cucumber

Do you know the days of the week?

try different cheeses

Make a coral reef
Use sponges, dishcloths and scourers

SONG (Tune: Twinkle, Twinkle Little Star)

See the donkey in its stall
"Eeyore! /ee/-/or/!" is its call.

ACTION: Put your hands on your head like a donkey's ears. Point them up for *ee* and down for *or*.

sheep

speech

Build a Small World

street

or

Tongue Twister
The dormouse was sore and sat indoors feeling poorly.

Make a storm picture
smudge the paint with your fingers

stick on pasta to make lightening

seashore

Look and Draw
Some storms make incredible patterns in the sky. Try drawing one.

storm

Do you prefer playing indoors or outdoors?

Do you ever use public transport? Find out if it helps the environment to use our own cars less and travel together more.

trains   buses

What public transport services do you have where you live?

orchestra

fork

Make a giant storybook
Cover strong card with brown material to make the covers.

Use a cold, wet teabag to stain the inside pages and make them look old

```
s a t i p n
c k e h r m d
g o u l f b
ai j oa ie ee or
```

Is the sound /ee/ or /or/?

ee   or

Make words
for, fork, corn, horn
sort, torn, born, cork, fort
sport, storm, stork

stork

How many storms can you name?

tropical
thunder
hurricane
typhoon
tornado

Z

freeze ice cubes with fresh fruit

Time how long it takes water to freeze into ice cubes.

sneeze

jigsaw puzzle

Make a Beehive

Paint an egg carton yellow.

Make bees from black and yellow pom-poms with coloured cellophane for the wings.

ZZZZZZ

blaze

Zesty Lime Sponge cake
Ingredients:
175g soft margarine
175g golden sugar
3 eggs beaten
2 limes zested and juiced
175g self-raising flour
200g lemon & lime marmalade
150ml double cream
1 heaped tablespoon icing sugar & a little extra for dusting

Method:
Preheat oven to 180c / gas 4.
Beat together the margarine and sugar until smooth and creamy. Gradually add the flour and eggs a little at a time and keep whisking until smooth.
Whisk in the lime juice and zest.
Divide the batter into 2 portions and pour into 2 greased and lined 20cm cake tins.
Bake for 30 mins.
Allow sponges to cool, then spread the marmalade on top of one sponge. Whisk the cream and icing sugar together and smooth over the marmalade. Place the other sponge on top and dust with icing sugar.

Role Play
Be a zookeeper who takes care of lots of animals.

Make zigzag patterns
Cut paper zigzags, or try painting or drawing them

Water Tray

Add baking soda, vinegar and food colouring to water and watch it fizz!

Fizzy Water

Tongue Twister
The amazing wizard sneezed and wheezed as he snoozed.

lazy

Make a zebra

Cover cardboard tubes with white paper and draw black stripes. Roll some card to make the legs and add pom-poms and eyes.

snooze

What size shoes do you wear?

Look and Draw
Look at the horizon and draw or paint what you can see.

horizon

zombie

SONG (Tune: Did You Ever See a Lassie?)

Did you ever hear a bee buzz,
  a bee buzz,
    a bee buzz?
Did you ever hear a bee buzz, "/zzz/!", like this?

ACTION: Put your arms out at your sides and flap them like a bee, saying zzzzzz.

Make a zoo

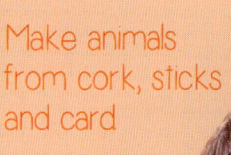
Make animals from cork, sticks and card

z

find out about mangel-wurzels

Mangel-wurzels are root vegetables similar to beetroots and we can eat the roots and the leaves. They make good food for farm animals.

grizzly bear

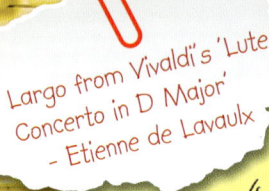
zany

Largo from Vivaldi's 'Lute Concerto in D Major' - Etienne de Lavaulx

listen to someone playing the zither

Build a Small World

zoo

Think of some questions and hold a quiz for your friends.

sizzling

the animal kingdom

Find out about zoology. If you are a zoologist, you learn all about animal life in the animal kingdom. Where animals live, how they live and how they survive. Would you like this job?

Find out about Brazil

s a t i p n
c k e h r m d
g o u l f b
ai j oa ie ee or
z

Choose which word

zap
sip
unzip

run
sun
fun

bad
mad
sad

Make words

zip, zest, zit, unzip, zap
buzz, jazz, fizz, zigzag

make a wizard's hat

W

try waffles with different toppings

Try:
fresh fruit
cream
nuts
chocolate
syrup

wash

world

Make Windmills

Stick your windmill on an ice lolly stick

Start with four triangle shapes and fold each left corner to the top point.

wwww

washing machine

Welsh Cakes
Ingredients:

300g plain flour
1 teaspoon baking powder
large pinch of nutmeg
pinch of ground cinnamon
100g caster sugar plus extra for dusting
50g soft butter diced
50g soft lard diced
1 egg beaten
100g dried currants

Method:

Sieve the flour and baking powder into a large bowl and stir in the nutmeg, cinnamon and sugar.
Add the butter and lard and rub with your fingers until the mixture resembles breadcrumbs.
Mix in the egg and currants and fold into a dough.
Wrap the dough in cling film and refrigerate for 30 mins.
Roll the dough and cut 10cm rounds.
Heat a greased frying pan and cook each round for 2 mins on each side until nicely golden.
Remove from pan and dust each side with sugar whilst the cake is still warm. Eat warm too!

Role Play
Be a waiter or a waitress in a busy restaurant.

Make a werewolf picture

W

Make a web

Use silver thread or white paint and sprinkle silver glitter over the web before it dries.

whisk

wand

Go for a walk.

Build a Small World

wedding

wind chimes are relaxing and good for meditation

listen to wind chime sounds

whistle

wings

Find out how much things weigh. You can use digital weighing scales or traditional balancing ones.

What are the heaviest and lightest objects you have weighed?

s a t i p n c k e
h r m d g o u l f
b ai j oa ie ee
or z w

Draw things that have the sound /w/.

Make words

wet, win, wig, web
went, wind, west, will
wait, weep, weed, well
week, worn, swim

paint using watercolours

Use magic wax crayons

Fill a piece of paper with coloured wax crayons. Paint over the top with black watercolour paint. When dry, use a coin to scratch a picture.

Write a secret message with wax. Reveal the message by painting over the top of it with black paint.

weeping willow

watch

weasel

How do we eat wheat?

crackers

bread

cereal

pasta

Talk about what worries you.

Talk about what you wish for.

Talk about how to reduce waste.

BOOKS TO READ

The Huge Bag of Worries
 - Virginia Ironside

The Storm Whale
 - Benji Davies

Elmer's Weather
 - David McKee

Wanda's Washing Machine
 - Anna McQuinn

William's Winter Wish
 - Gillian Shields

All the Water in the World
 - George Ella Lyon & Katherine Tillotson

ng

what are our lungs for?
We need our lungs to breathe. They fill with air when we take a breath.

Smoking damages our lungs and makes them dirty.

Farmers spread animal dung on fields to help crops grow.

dung

Make a Weightlifter

Use pom-poms and a paper straw for the weights

Use ice lolly sticks for the body and a pom-pom for the head

Cut out clothes from coloured paper or foam

ng...

gang

Lamingtons
Ingredients:

70g plain flour
35g cornflour
1/2 teaspoon baking powder
3 eggs beaten
50g sugar
2 tablespoons milk
1 tablespoon butter

Topping:
chocolate icing
120g shredded coconut

Method:

Preheat oven to 165c / gas 3.
Sift the flour, cornflour and baking powder into a large mixing bowl. In a separate bowl, beat the eggs with an electric whisk until thick and foamy and then add the sugar a tablespoon at a time. Continue to beat the eggs for 6 mins until thick
Meanwhile heat milk and butter in a microwave for 30 seconds and leave to cool slightly Add the flour mixture and butter mixture to the eggs and gently fold until mixed together. Add to a greased and lined 8" cake tin and bake for 20 mins.
Cut the cake into 12 squares, dip each square into chocolate icing and cover with coconut.

Role Play
Be a king ruling a kingdom.

OBJECTS TO COLLECT
spring
ring
sling
gong
kangaroo
string

taste different vegetables

carrots

mushrooms

onions

peas

sweetcorn

potatoes

Tongue Twister
The vegetarian vampire ate vegetables with vitamins.

How many other different vegetables do you know?

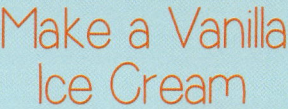
voyage

Make a Vanilla Ice Cream

Dip cotton balls in paint to make the ice cream and sprinkle with glitter and sequins.

vaccine

Look and Draw
Look at a vase of flowers and draw the different leaves and petals.

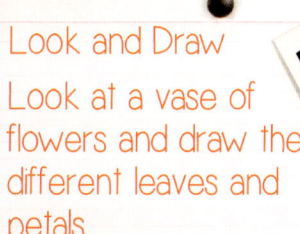
vase

visitor

SONG (Tune: Go in and Out the Windows)

Drive Vic's van round the village.
Drive Vic's van round the village.
Drive Vic's van round the village
- /v/ - /v/ - /v/ - /v/ - /v/

Make a Valentine's Card

Make tissue paper roses with 5 squares of tissue paper in a pile. Fold them in a consertina, staple the centre and then pull each layer towards the centre.

ACTION: Pretend to be driving along in a van, saying *vvvvvv*.

113

V

find out about artist Vincent van Gogh

Van Gogh was a Dutch painter born in 1853 who created around 2,100 pieces of art. He famously cut off part of his own left ear.

victory

vacuum

'The Four Seasons' Violin Concertos - Vivaldi

listen to violin music

Build a Small World

village

Sing a verse of your favourite song.

jellyfish, scorpion, frog, spider, pufferfish, snake

Find out about venomous creatures. Why do they have venom? Is it to kill their prey or to defend themselves? Do they usually bite or sting?

Add a vowel

s a t i p n
c k e h r m d
g o u l f b
ai j oa ie ee or
z w ng v

a e i o u

p_n p_n p_n
h_t h_t h_t
b_t b_t b_t

Make words
van, vat, vain, valid
vet, vent, vest, vivid
invent

Explode a Volcano

create lava with red paint, vinegar and baking soda

oo

try hula hooping
How long can you spin a hoop on your waist?

Can you spin more than one hula-hoop at a time?

Maroon is a dark reddish purple colour. What things can be maroon?
cherries
horse chestnuts
grapes
roses

Make a Cuckoo Clock

oo-oo, oo-oo!

Make a cuckoo from pom-poms and a craft feather.

Attach it to the clock with a consertina-folded piece of card

moon

igloo

Gooseberry Cake
Ingredients:
225g soft butter
225g golden caster sugar
200g self-raising flour
50g ground almond
4 eggs beaten
1 orange zested and juiced
225g fresh gooseberries, washed, topped & tailed
150g caster sugar

Method:
Preheat oven to 180c / gas 4.
Whisk together the butter, sugar, flour, orange zest and ground almonds until smooth. Add 3/4 of the gooseberries and mix well.
Pour mixture into a greased and lined 25 x 25cm square baking tin.
Gently push in the remaining gooseberries and bake for 30 mins.
Meanwhile, sieve the orange juice and mix with the sugar to make a syrup. Remove the cake from the oven and spoon syrup over the top. Return to the oven for 5 mins.

Role Play
Be customers in a tearoom having afternoon tea

OBJECTS TO COLLECT
toothbrush
boots
balloon
spoon
wool
book

discover types of edible mushrooms

porcini

honey

aspen bolete

russula

champignon

Never pick and eat wild mushrooms in case they are poisonous.

scooter

stool

Make a mushroom house

Paint a paper bowl and attach it to a carboard tube or pot.

Stick pom-poms on for decoration and draw a door.

Make a rooftop picture

Cut rooftop outlines from black paper and edge them with silver glitter to look like the reflection of the moon.

Stick a white circle moon and some stars onto a dark blue sky.

SONG (Tune: Go In and Out the Windows)

Who wants to be a cuckoo?
Who wants to be a cuckoo?
Who wants to be a cuckoo?
/oo/-/oo/, /oo/-/oo/, /oo/-/oo/!

ACTION: Move your head back and forth like the cuckoo in a cuckoo clock, calling *oo-oo, oo-oo*. (*oo* as in book, *oo* as in moon)

moose

scoop

Build a Small World

swimming pool

oo

Tongue Twister
In moonlight the spooky witch zoomed on her broom.

Design some boots 
Stick on anything you like to make your boots stand out.

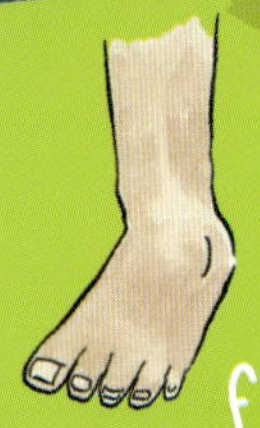

foot

Look and Draw
Look at the pattern of a plant's roots and draw what you see.

roots

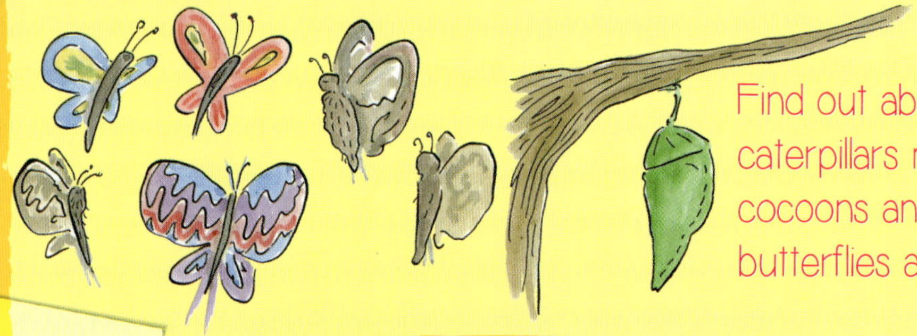

Find out about how caterpillars make cocoons and turn into butterflies and moths.

hood

bamboo

Mood music is meant to create a mood or feeling. Try creating a calm mood with music.

listen to mood music

s a t i p n
c k e h r m d
g o u l f b
ai j oa ie ee or
z w ng v oo

long /oo/ or short /oo/?

Make little /oo/ words
wool, hook, book, foot, wood
look, good, woof, stood

Make long /oo/ words
boot, zoo, root, cool, food
fool, soon, spoon, stool

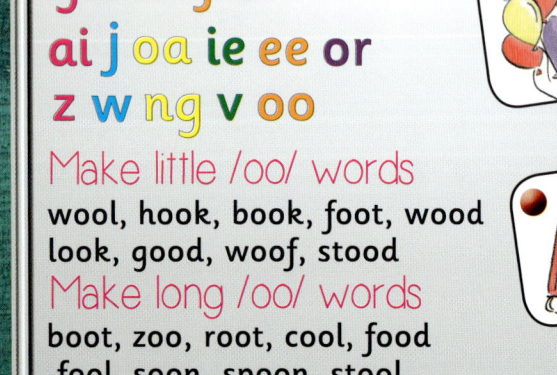

try drawing cartoons

try different types of noodles

udon noodles
wonton noodles
soba noodles
vermicelli noodles
egg noodles
rice noodles

Compare their shape and thickness. Do they taste different?

toadstool

rooster

roof

Make a wooden spoon family

Cut out clothes from card or fabric. Stick on buttons or beads. Use wool for hair and draw on faces. You can stick on googly eyes

Make a moon

Start with a circle of card and stick pieces of cereal onto it.
Cover the moon with silver paint or spray.

BOOKS TO READ

Goodnight Moon
 - Margaret Wise Brown

White Boots
 - Noel Streatfeild

Room on the Broom
 - Julia Donaldson

Emily's Balloon
 - Komako Sakai

Truman's Loose Tooth
 - Kristine Wurm

Little Red Riding Hood
 - Traditional

Only One Woof
 - James Herriot

Talk about the mood you are in.

Talk about what you enjoy in school.

Talk about your favourite food.

y

make a collection of yellow things

How many yellow fruits and vegetables can you think of?

Make a Yogurt Dessert

Start with natural yogurt and add ingredients for flavour and texture.

TRY ADDING:
jam or honey
maple syrup
vanilla extract
fresh fruit
cinnamon
granola
cereal
chocolate

yyyy

yummy

yogurt

Name all the months of the year.

Yogurt Cake

Ingredients:

150ml unsweetened plain yogurt
200g self-raising flour
150g sugar
100ml mild olive oil
3 eggs
splash of vanilla extract
pinch of salt
handful of chopped fruit

Method:

Preheat oven to 180c / gas 4.
Pour all the ingredients, except the fruit, into a large bowl and whisk until nicely combined and smooth.
Pour half the mixture into a greased and lined standard loaf tin.
Press in half of the fruit.
Pour in the rest of the mixture and then press in the rest of the fruit.
Bake for 45-60 mins until nicely golden.

Make yoga poses

Triangle pose | Down dog pose | Warrior pose | Boat pose | Cobra pose

Bend pipe cleaners into people doing yoga poses. There are lots of poses to choose from including: triangle pose, downward dog pose, warrior pose, boat pose and cobra pose.

make your own custard from egg yolks

YOU WILL NEED:
500ml milk
4 egg yolks
1 tsp vanilla extract
1 tbs cornflour

Mix all the ingredients in a bowl except the milk. Heat the milk until it's almost boiling, then whisk it into the mixture. Heat and stir the custard until it thickens.

Have fun separating the egg yolk from the egg white!

Tongue Twister
Yesterday the yellow yacht reached your yard.

yap

yew tree

Role Play
Be a Yeoman of the Guard, defending the Queen in London.

Play a YES and NO game. You must answer questions without using the words YES or NO.

Look and Draw
Draw a picture of yourself with your favourite person, animal or object.

yourself

yowling

SONG (Tune: Apples and Bananas)
I like to eat, eat, eat, yogurt and bananas.
I like to eat, eat, eat, yogurt and bananas.
I like to eat, eat, eat, yogurt and bananas.
-/y/-/y/-/y/
-/y/-/y/!

Make a yo-yo
Draw around your hand and cut out the shape

To make the yo-yo, cut a short strip of card, curl it into a circle and stick the ends together. Now stick two circles of card onto each side.
Decorate the circles
Wind thread or string around the yo-yo and then tie it onto the middle finger of your hand

ACTION: Pretend to eat yogurt from a spoon, saying y, y, y, y.

y

Make bread with yeast

You need flour, water and yeast to make bread. It is the yeast that makes the bread rise.

yawn

yell

She Taught Me to Yodel - Frank Ifield

listen to yodelling

Build a Small World

yuletide

yarn

Listen to the song 'Yellow Submarine' by The Beatles.

Find out about the myth of the Yeti, also known as the 'Abominable Snowman', from Himalayan folklore. It is said to be an ape-like creature that lives in the mountains.

Draw a picture of what you think the Yeti might look like.

which sounds do you know?

s a t i p n
ck e h r m d
g o u l f b
ai j oa ie ee or
z w ng v oo
y

yes   no

Make words

yes, yap, yak, yam
yet, yen, yum
yell, yelp, yuck

draw a yellow submarine

Make a yacht

Cut a paper plate in half and colour it in. Use a straw for the mast and triangles of paper for the sail and flag

Cut out a ring to stick on the front.

yard

yeast

Discover what young animals are called

young cow	young deer	young goat	young tiger
CALF	FAWN	KID	CUB

young kangaroo	young dog	young sheep	young cat
JOEY	PUPPY	LAMB	KITTEN

BOOKS TO READ

Dear Yeti
- James Kwan

The Little Leprechaun Who Loved Yellow
- Sally Huss

Yak Yuk
- Michelle Robinson

Yummy Yucky
- Leslie Patricelli

I Dare You Not to Yawn
- Hélène Boudreau

Talk about what makes you yawn.

Talk about what you did yesterday.

Talk about yourself.

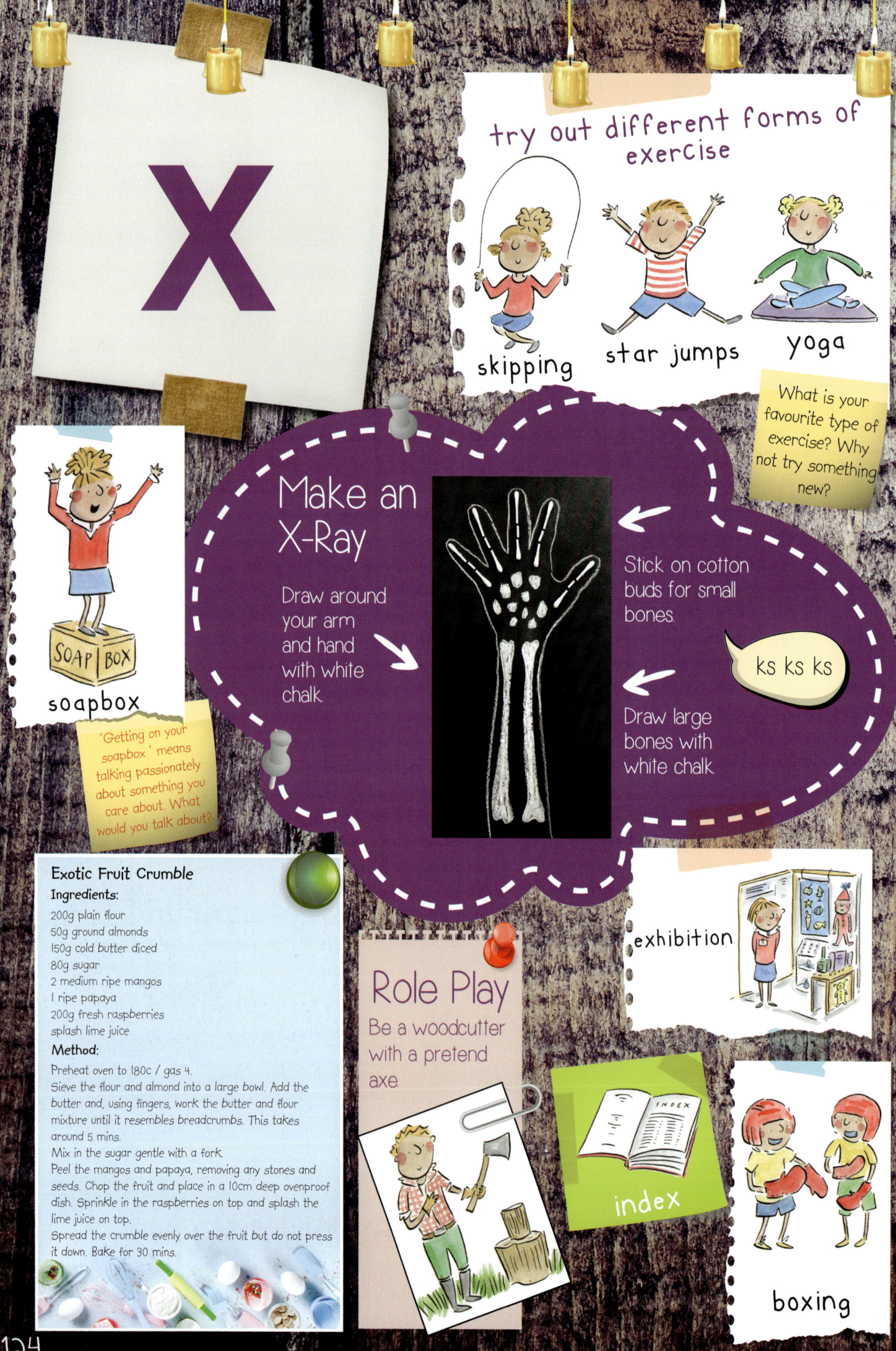

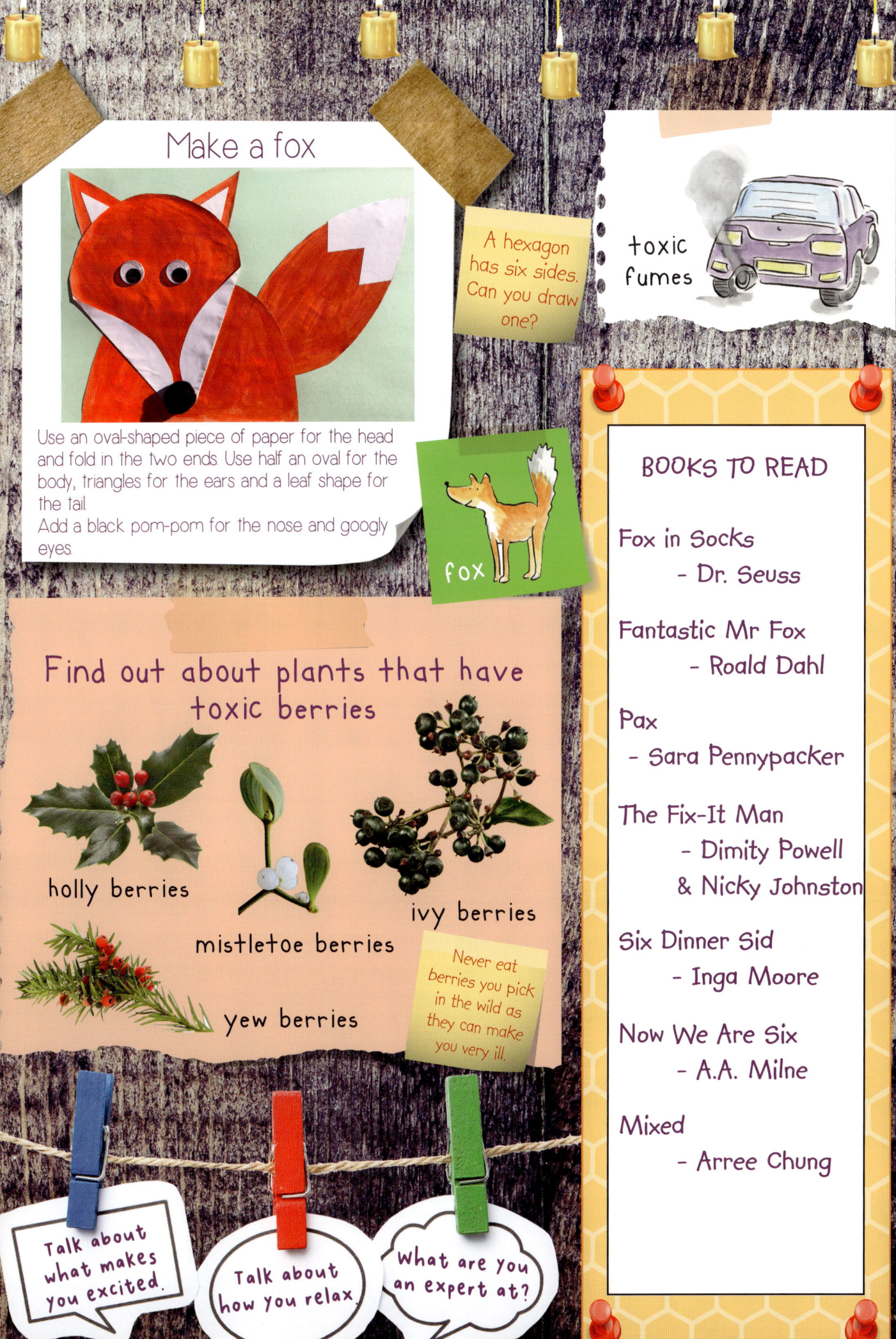

try eating Chinese food

chow mein
dumplings
egg fried rice
wonton soup
spring rolls

Make a chimney

Paint a tissue box with a brick design and use cotton balls for smoke.

roast some chestnuts

Learn to play chess.

Make a chick

Put a large blob of yellow paint in the middle of your paper and use an old toothbrush to brush the paint out to make a feathered effect.

Cut out a beak and feet from orange paper.

SONG (Tune: Merrily We Roll Along)

Trains are chugging up the hill.
/ch/-/ch/-/ch/, /ch/-/ch/-/ch/.
Trains are chugging up the hill.
/ch/-/ch/-/ch/ choo, choo!

 ACTION: Move your arms at your sides like a steam train, saying ch, ch, ch, ch.

chipmunk

chase

Challenge yourself to do something new.

Build a Small World

chicken coop

129

Tongue Twister

The cheeky chipmunk chuckled and chased the chicken.

Print cherries

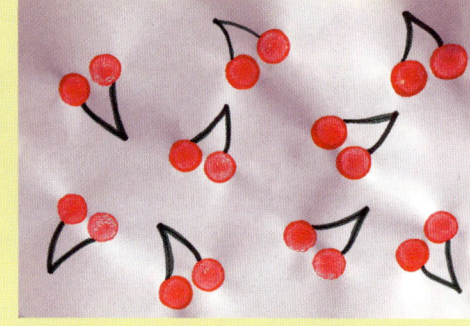

Use the end of a cork to print cherries and then paint in the stalks.

charger

Look and Draw
Look at the beautiful colours on this bird and try drawing one.

chaffinch

Think of ways you can raise money for charity. There are always charities that need help.

sponsored read   toy sale

church

chuckle

Try using chopsticks

chain

cheeky

Hear the /ch/ at the end of

bench   hutch   itch
torch   lunch

```
s a t i p n
c k e h r m d
g o u l f b
ai j oa ie ee or
z w ng v oo
y x ch
```

Make words
chin, rich, chop, chat, much
chill, chest, chain, chimp
torch, bench, speech, bunch

match the sounds

ch	c	ch	h
ai	i	a	ai
ee	ee	e	
ie	e	i	ie
oa	o	oa	a
or	or	r	o

make a chart

sh

Tongue Twister
Shall we share the shade in the shelter of the shrub?

Design and make a shield 
Cut a shield shape from a piece of card and cover it with silver foil. Decorate your shield with lines and pictures that you like.

Collect shiny things.

Look and Draw
On a sunny day, draw around someone's shadow on the ground with chalk.

shadow

Look at different ways that sheds can be used. What would you use your shed for?

tool shed   tea shed

shopping

shelves

shade

shawl

Hear the /sh/ at the end of

fish   brush   push

mash

```
s a t i p n
c k e h r m d
g o u l f b
ai j oa ie ee or
z w ng v oo
y x ch sh
```

Make words
shop, shed, shelf, shook
short, shall, shrimp, shin
brush, wish, rush, blush

Solve animal anagrams

ee sh p

ee b

s a t g

make a shape picture

discover types of shrub

camellia

fatsia

hydrangea

lavender

poinsettia

Showtunes are songs from musical theatre. Discover your favourite.

listen to showtunes

shave

Make shell people

Use different shaped shells to make figures.

You can also use little stones for detail and a piece of driftwood or a stick for them to stand on.

BOOKS TO READ

Shhh! Don't Wake the Royal Baby!
- Martha Mumford

Shaun the Sheep
- Martin Howard

Ballet Shoes
- Noel Streatfeild

The Shark in the Dark
- Peter Bently

My Shadow
- Robert Louis Stevenson

Seashells by the Seashore
- Marianne Berkes

Talk about why it's good to share.

Talk about your favourite place to shop.

Talk about when you feel shy.

what is your favourite theme park ride?

boat swings, bumper cars, carousel, Ferris wheel, roller coaster

throat

thread

Make a thinking head

Start with a cut out silhouette of your head. Then cut out what you are thinking about today and stick it on top of the head

Think of someone you could make a thank you bouquet for.

Make a thank you bouquet

Fold a rectangle of green card in half and cut slits from the folded side, leaving a gap at the end. Curve the open end round on itself and stick together. Cut out flowers from coloured card and stick them onto the folded ends.

SONG (Tune: Did You Ever See a Lassie?)

Did you ever hear a rude clown make this sound and that sound?
Did you ever hear a rude clown say /th/-/th/, /th/-/th/?

ACTION: Pretend to be a rude clown. Stick out your tongue a little for *th* (as in *this*) and further for *th* (as in *thumb*).

throne

thumb

Build a Small World

theatre

137

th

Tongue Twister
Three thousand thunderstorms made thick throbbing thuds.

Make a thunderstorm

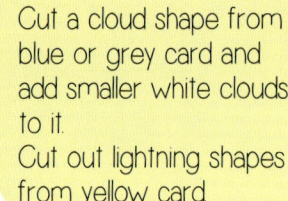

Cut a cloud shape from blue or grey card and add smaller white clouds to it.
Cut out lightning shapes from yellow card
Stick pieces of ribbon to the back of the cloud to make rain.

thermometer

Look and Draw
Look at the pattern of feathers on a thrush and try to draw it.

thrush

play therapy

Talk about how therapy can help children who are upset or troubled. Talking or playing with someone who understands can help.

Share your worries and troubles with someone.

thirsty

A theremin is an electronic musical instrument.

listen to theremin music

thief

label /sh/, /ch/ or /th/

s a t i p n
c k e h r m d
g o u l f b
ai j oa ie ee or
z w ng v oo
y x ch sh th

Make voiced /th/ words
this, that, then, them, than with, within

Make unvoiced /th/ words
thin, tenth, thing, thump moth, teeth, north, strength

Are you afraid of thunder?

Can you think of things that are THICK and THIN?

thorns

discover different thermometers

- placed in the armpit to measure body temperature
- used to measure the temperature of food
- placed under the tongue to measure body temperature
- placed on the wall to measure weather temperature

thistle

Find out how long it takes for something frozen to thaw. Try different objects.

Make a thistle

Handmade craft paper has a good texture for giving a 'prickly' effect. Use some purple handmade paper, make cuts in it and roll so that the cut pieces can fan out.

Use green card for the stem and green tissue paper for the leaves.

thunderstorm

Make thumbprint people

Make thumbprints with ink if you have it, or you can use paint. When dry, use a pen to add arms, legs and faces that bring your characters to life.

Talk about going to the theatre.

Talk about what you are thinking.

Why is it important to say thank you?

BOOKS TO READ

Thumbelina
- Hans Christian Andersen

Hand, Hand, Fingers, Thumb
- Al Perkins

Thunder Cake
- Patricia Polacco

The Most Magnificent Thing
- Ashley Spires

Bear Says "Thank You"
- Michael Dahl

QUADRUPLE: what comes in fours?

ELEMENTS
water
fire
air
earth

CARD SUITS
spades
diamonds
hearts
clubs

CARDINAL DIRECTIONS
north
east
south
west

SEASONS
winter
spring
summer
autumn

1
2
3
4

Can you count in 4's?

Hear the /qu/ in

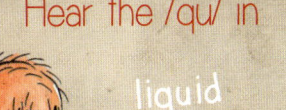

squirrel
liquid
squid
equator

Make clocks to show the time

secure the hands with a split pin so that they can move

quarter to the hour

quarter past the hour

SONG (Tune: The Wheels on the Bus)

The duck in the pond quacks
"/qu/-/qu/-/qu/,"
"/qu/-/qu/-/qu/,"
"/qu/-/qu/-/qu/,"
The duck in the pond quacks
"/qu/-/qu/-/qu/,"
all around the pond.

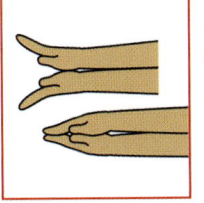

ACTION: Make a duck's beak with your hands and open and close it, saying qu, qu, qu, qu.

quick

Build a Small World

quacking ducks

141

qu

Tongue Twister
The quarrelsome queen questioned the quality of the quill.

Make quills
Use a toothbrush to paint a feather effect. Stick a coloured straw in the middle and draw on a nib.

Before pens were invented, quills were dipped in ink and used for writing. They were usually made from goose feathers.

Look and Draw
Quilts are made from squares of different designs. Try drawing one.

quiet

quilt

quarry

sand   gravel   rocks

Find out about what happens in a quarry. Sand, gravel, rocks and other minerals are removed to be used for building things.

A quiver is the name for the container that holds arrows.

quest

questionnaire

Make a quiver
Paint a plastic cup in a bright design and attach a ribbon to it for a strap.

Make arrows from sticks or straws with feathered card tops.

```
s  a  t  i  p  n
ck e  h  r  m  d
g  o  u  l  f  b
ai j  oa ie ee or
z  w  ng v  oo
y  x  ch sh th
qu
```

Make words
quiz, quick, quit, quilt
queen, quest, quack, quiver
squid, liquid, quail

Is the sound /qu/ or /ck/?

quench

Write a quiz for your friends and family. Think of questions based on something you enjoy.

make a quartz collection

- amethyst
- citrine
- smoky quartz
- rose quartz

listen to quena music

Colors of the Wind
- Wuauquikuna
Quena de los Andes
- Raul Olarte

qualification

Have you ever taken an exam to gain a qualification? For a musical instrument, a sport or another hobby?

queasy

Make pizza quarters

Use circles of card for the pizza base and tomato sauce. Cut out paper toppings to stick onto the pizza

Each quarter should be the same size.

BOOKS TO READ

Quick Quack Quentin
- Kes Gray & Jim Field

The Queen's Hat
- Steve Antony

The Name Quilt
- Phyllis Root

The Quiet Book
- Deborah Underwood

The Queen's Knickers
- Nicholas Allan

Talk about a quarrel you have had.

Talk about why you should try not to quit.

Talk about what you can do quickly.

ou

Tongue Twister
She was proud of the bouncey couch in the lounge of the house.

Make a mouth
Cut out the mouth shape from red and pink card. Add a red tongue and stick white mini marshmallows around the inside for the teeth.

trout

Look and Draw
Look at a seed sprouting and draw it at each stage as it grows.

sprout

Can you count to ten in another language?

A noun is a person, place or object. Can you think of a noun?

Find out about animals that have a pouch. They are called marsupials and they carry their young in their pouches.

bandicoot, koala, kangaroo, opossum

couch

spout

Make a mouse
Start with a triangle of black paper and fold the top down to make the head. Then add ears, whiskers, a tail, and a pink pom-pom for the nose.

Add googly eyes.

s a t i p n
c k e h r m d
g o u l f b
ai j oa ie ee or
z w ng v oo
y x ch sh th
qu ou

Solve the anagrams
sh i f
u d ck
oa d t

Make words
out, loud, shout, cloud, spout
mouth, count, couch, south
found, round, ground, hound

make a chalky mountain sunset picture.

Can you hear the same sound?

royal   boy   joy   toy

Try embroidery

Start with a simple embroidery set with instructions.

Never eat anything you pick outside without first checking it is safe.

Soil has microbes in it that help to make you feel relaxed and calm. That's why gardening can be good for you.

soil

find out about poisonous flowers

daffodil   marigold   foxglove   oleander

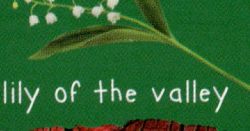

lily of the valley

These flowers are only harmful if you eat them. Take care that your pets don't nibble on them either.

SONG (Tune: Old MacDonald)

The sailors met upon the sea,
/oi/-/oi/, /oi/-/oi/, /oi/.
They found some oil way down deep.
/oi/-/oi/, "Ship ahoy!"

 ACTION: Cup your hands around your mouth as if you are hailing a passing boat, and say oi, ship ahoy!

choice

embroidery

Build a Small World →

oil rig

149

find cuboids

← book
brick →
← cabinet
↑ wafer
↑ box

Draw the noises you can hear. People talking? Traffic? Birds singing?

listen to noises around you

moisturise

Make some foil art

Draw a simple picture and then trace over the pencil lines with a glue gun. When the glue is dry, use a craft glue to stick a piece of foil over the top and press down firmly. Then use felt tip pens to add colour to the foil.

BOOKS TO READ

Mr. Noisy
   - Roger Hargreaves

Boing
   - Adam Russell-Owen

Too Much Noise
   - Ann McGovern

Oil Spill!
   - Melvin Berger

Boing Boing
   - Alexander McCall Smith & Zoe Persico

Talk about something you avoid doing.

Talk about a club or group you'd like to join.

Talk about when you are noisy.

ue

make a collection of blue things

The letters 'ue' can say /y-oo/ or /oo/. Listen carefully to 'cue' and 'blue' - can you hear the difference?

Try making blue by mixing green and yellow paint.

Make a Pointing Hand

Draw on card, cut out and colour.

ue ue ue ue

You can use this for fun games or for when you have circle time and take turns to talk.

cruel

Blueberry Muffin Cake

Ingredients:

225g butter at room temperature
175g golden sugar
4 eggs beaten
225g plain flower
1 tablespoon baking powder
pinch of nutmeg
100g fresh blueberries

Method:

Preheat oven to 200c / gas 6.
Whisk the butter and sugar together at high speed for 30 seconds. Then add 2 tablespoons of the flour and slowly whisk in the eggs. When well combined, whisk for another 2 mins.
Sieve and fold in the rest of the flour, baking powder and nutmeg.
Pour the mixture into a greased and lined 20cm cake tin and then press in the blueberries. Refrigerate for an hour.
Place the cold dough in the oven and bake for 40 mins.

Role Play

Be part of a rescue team, such as a firefighter, and save lives.

Make a treasure hunt with lots of clues. Then ask someone to solve the clues and find the treasure.

avenue

argue

ue

Make a Statue of Liberty costume

Cut out the rim of a paper plate and stick triangles around the top to make the crown.

The torch can be made from a cardboard tube with the inside of a pot of cheese stuck on top of it. Use coloured tissue for the flames.

Look and Draw
Look closely at a bluebird and try drawing and colouring one.

bluebird

sports stadium

conference hall

theatre

Find out about different venues where events take place. What kind of events happen in each venue?

Are you influenced by anyone? Is there someone you watch and think 'I want to be like you'? Talk about how influence can be good and bad.

cue

Tongue Twister
It's true that the bluebird flew to the statue in the avenue.

Play a game of musical statues. Dance to music. When the music stops you must freeze like a statue. If you move you are out!

Make your own glue

Mix half a cup of flour and approximately half a cup of water in a bowl. Add the water slowly, stirring all the time, until the consistency is gooey and not too watery. Finally stir a pinch of salt. You glue paste is ready to use.

s a t i p n
c k e h r m d
g o u l f b
ai j oa ie ee or
z w ng v oo
y x ch sh th
qu ou oi ue

Make words

due, cue, fuel, rescue, clue glue, true, value, statue

Read and draw.

- a big statue
- three ducks
- a green frog

er

Make a gingerbread man

To make gingerbread dough you need: 225g plain flour, 2 tsp bicarbonate of soda, 1 tsp ground ginger, 1 tsp cinnamon, 50g butter, 100g soft brown sugar, 100g golden syrup.

Heat the butter, sugar and syrup until dissolved and add to the sieved dry ingredients to make a dough. Refrigerate for 30 mins before rolling and cutting your gingerbread. Decorate with icing.

butterfly

elderly

Make a Whisk

Bend three pipe cleaners to make the end of the whisk.

er-er-er-er

Use another pipe cleaner for the handle.

Wrap another pipe cleaner around the handle.

Write a letter to someone.

Butter Cookies

Ingredients:
110g softened butter
70g sugar
1 egg yolk
splash of vanilla extract
140g plain flour
chocolate and sprinkles

Method:
Preheat oven to 180c / gas 4.
Use an electric mixer to whisk the butter and sugar together until creamy. Then whisk in the egg yolk and vanilla extract.
Sieve the flour into the mixture and fold in well.
Spoon the dough into a piping bag with a large star-shaped spout and pipe 12 rounds onto a greased baking tray. Leave enough space between them for them to expand.
Refrigerate for 30 mins before baking for 15 mins.
Allow to cool and then dip half of each cookie into some melted chocolate. Add sprinkles.

Role Play

Be a nursery school teacher, looking after very young children

Make a dreamcatcher

Wrap coloured cotton around the rim of a plastic lid to make the top.

Thread beads onto lengths of cotton and tie them to the lid, adding feathers at the bottom.

Hang your dreamcatcher above your bed

er

Tongue Twister
Remember to never ever walk under a builder's ladder.

Make a summer picture.
Use brightly coloured paper and use buttons for flowers, matchsticks for a deckchair, a bottle lid for the sun and cotton balls for clouds.

Look and Draw
Ferns have very feathery leaves. Look carefully and try drawing one.

fern

Find out about the legend of mermaids. They have the upper body of a human and the tail of a fish and are sometimes said to cause storms or shipwrecks.

builder

weightlifter

burger

Make a watermelon fan
Use half of a paper plate and decorate it to look like a slice of watermelon. Stick a straw or stick behind it to make a handle.

```
s a t i p n
c k e h r m d
g o u l f b
ai j oa ie ee or
z w ng v oo
y x ch sh th
qu ou oi ue er
```

Match the word to the picture.

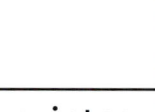
winter

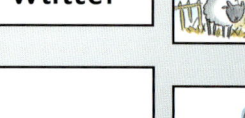
farmer

Make words
her, herd, ever, fern
perfect, offer, clever, term
number, silver, letter, winter
river, thunder, shiver, mister

letter

cleaner

Find out which animals hibernate in the winter.

ar

Make a decorative jar
Wash an empty jar and fill it with shells and miniature battery-operated llights to make an attractive decoration.

Make a Doctor's Bag
Cut out the bag from blue card.

Stick lids, cotton balls, ice lolly sticks and other items inside.

barbecue
(British English)
ar

make a shark
Use an old sock and stick cardboard fins onto it. Sew on black buttons for the eyes.

Make a Seal
Use string for whiskers.

Use paper plates painted grey for the body.

(American English)
ar ar ar ar

Marble Cake
Ingredients:
100g warm butter
80ml vegetable oil
140g icing sugar
1 tablespoon maple syrup
splash vanilla extract
3 eggs beaten
110g plain flour
40g corn flour
1/2 teaspoon baking powder
zest from 1/2 lemon
10g cocoa
2 tablespoons milk

Method:
Preheat oven to 190c / gas 5.
Whisk together the warm butter, oil, sugar, syrup and vanilla. When smooth, whisk in the eggs one at a time. Then slowly sieve in the flours, baking powder and lemon, whisking continuously. Then whisk for another 5 mins.
In a small bowl, mix the cocoa and milk into a paste. Spoon 1/4 of it into the cake mixture and mix until smooth.
Pour a layer of the mixture into a greased 1 litre loaf tin and then blob some chocolate paste on top. Continue layering the cake mixture and the chocolate paste, finishing with the cake mixture on top.
Take a fork, dig down into the cake mixture, and pull the fork in a wavy motion from one end to the other. Bake for 15 mins, then reduce the oven temperature to 175c/gas mark 4 and bake for a further 35 mins.

Role Play
Be a gardener taking care of lots of flowers and plants.

barn

How many star jumps can you do?

star jump

Discover types of lark

crested lark
rufous-tailed lark
horned lark
skylark
long-tailed meadowlark

There are approximately 90 different species of lark and they are a family of songbirds.

carp

dark

Design some marbles and give them good names.

make a marble collection

marbles have creative names that describe their colours:
comet
cat's eye
sunburst
swirl
dragonfly
watermelon

SONG (Tune: Camptown Races)
"Open wide," the doctor said.
/ar/! /ar/!
"Let me look at your sore throat.
Please say, '/ar/!'"
(British English)

SONG (Tune: Did You Ever See a Lassie?)
Did you ever hear a seal bark
A seal bark, a seal bark?
Did you ever hear a seal bark
/ar/-/ar/ - like this?
(American English)

arch

ACTION: Open your mouth wide, and say *ar*. (British English)

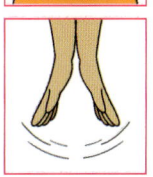
ACTION: Clap your hands loosely like a seal, and say *ar, ar, ar, ar.* (American English)

Build a Small World

garden party

ar

Tongue Twister
Far, far away, the charming star sparkled in the dark.

look in the sky for star constellations

harp

Look and Draw
Look at a whole garlic and some individual cloves and try to draw them.

garlic

A constellation is a pattern of stars, often representing an animal, mythological person or creature.

road   air   sea

Find out how cargo is carried by road, sea and air. Cargo can be any goods that need to be transported from one place to another.

Sing 'Twinkle Twinkle Little Star'.

sparkler

charms

Try bark rubbing
Rub a wax crayon onto paper held against a tree trunk.

Do different trees make different patterns?

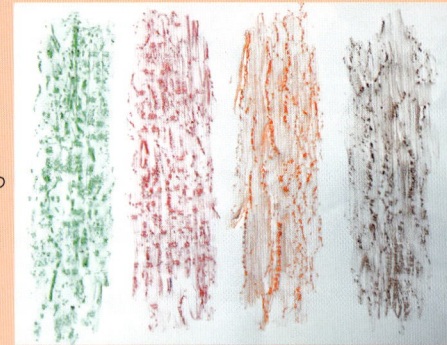

```
s a t i p n
c k e h r m d
g o u l f b
ai j oa ie ee or
z w ng v oo
y x ch sh th
qu ou oi ue er ar
```

Make words
arm, car, art, hard, farm
card, park, part, harm, star
start, shark, harsh, arch
sharp, farmer, artist, scarf

Read the word and match with the picture.

 car

 park

 garlic

carve

Spend some time gardening in the outdoors. You can clear weeds, plant seeds or prune plants when looking after a garden.

Make a starfish

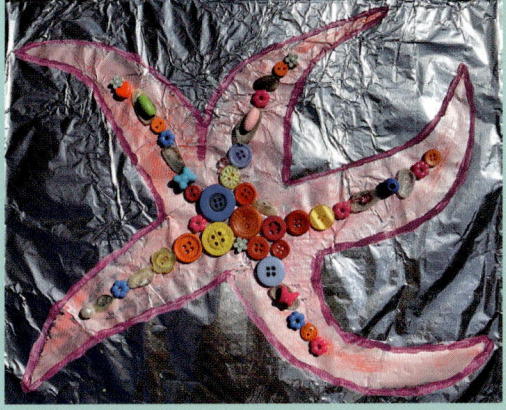

Cut a starfish shape from a piece of pink tissue paper and stick it onto a piece of foil.

Draw around the edges of the starfish with a pink felt-tip pen.

Stick buttons and beads onto the starfish.

Love Me Do
- The Beatles
The Midnight Cowboy Theme
- John Barry

listen to harmonica music

tartan

Try inventing your own fun arcade games involving skills such as throwing and hitting targets.

Make a fairground arcade game

Use cardboard tubes and rings to make a hoopla game. Throw the hoops from a distance and try to gain points by dropping them over a tube.

bark

BOOKS TO READ

Shark in the Park
- Nick Sharratt

The Secret Garden
- Frances Hodgson Burnett

The Owl Who Was Afraid of the Dark
- Jill Tomlinson

Star in the Jar
- Sam Hay
& Sarah Massini

Talk about something you find hard to do.

Talk about being afraid of the dark.

Talk about a party you have had.